Free Verse Editions
Edited by Jon Thompson

Also by Aby Kaupang

Radiant Tether

NOS (disorder, not otherwise specified) with Matthew Cooperman

Disorder 299.00 with Matthew Cooperman

Little "g" God Grows Tired of Me

Absence is Such a Transparent House

scenic fences | houses innumerable

& there's you still
thrill hour of the world to love

Aby Kaupang

Winner of the New Measure Poetry Prize

Parlor Press
Anderson, South Carolina
www.parlorpress.com

Parlor Press LLC, Anderson, South Carolina 29621

Library of Congress Cataloging-in-Publication Data on File

978-1-64317-358-0 (paperback)
978-1-64317-359-7 (pdf)
978-1-64317-360-3 (ePub)

1 2 3 4 5

Cover and interior design by David Blakesley
Cover photograph by James Sullivan

Parlor Press LLC is an independent publisher of scholarly and trade titles in print and multimedia formats. This book is available in paperback and ebook formats from Parlor Press on the web at https://parlorpress.com or through online and brick-and-mortar bookstores. For submission information or to find out about Parlor Press publications, write to Parlor Press, 3015 Brackenberry Drive, Anderson, South Carolina 29621, or email editor@parlorpress.com.

Contents

List of Figures

All images courtesy of the artist, James Sullivan.

for you
love
you
wending
in the nave
of the ampersand

the flesh   it rots in the air

the flesh   it rots in the air
rots the meat of the love of flesh
air is made of love   the meat is love
in the day   in inaction   action
is the love of doing the day   for meat
which rots in the air   love is meat to the bones
love is air
meat in the air is rotting   my love
is like air & elsewhere
he is like the love which is air
& elsewhere I am the meat

so it's clear to me—

valentine

Dear makers of the machine,

which 4:38am she clasps projects its blue light cartwheels of yellow fish dear to her palm wall pillow   my torso a temporary illuminant of bronze kelp Dear she is un-flinchingly tired & has raced the doctors & grandmas & won & is running in this circular blue night life a dolphin on the ceiling spills goldfishes fall

she opts

rainfall ocean heartbeat   Dear maker of this sound product had you ever intended the long fingered all night clasp of prehensile toes fingers on high wattage desir-able neighbors' walls or the sadness feeble of a rainforest memory fusel in a juvenile heart   she's in a cave in the bed   a combination of hours & nexts

        I too wish for the light

singing machine to press me a world other embraceable   your product is for good babies   babies with a weekly delay fat lipped tear swollen babies futuring in their parent's desires

I am nothing like your valentine baby darling all night you watch the industrial cir-cles of joyfish & have taken to placing them in surprising contexts   projector on the slatted turnshade   the natusi sofa   the shower's blue tile   water is the weapon of god

      oh god

Dear maker of that machine,

disability is a tree decorated in valentines & medical bills   it has placed the plum
visage across the cranium walls that keep us dark & shaken them & shaken me & we

the husband & I   our selves another narrative (written slowly to interject her story
only when she is breathing stooling or sleeping & in her world these are rarely found
rubies) he is snoozing roiling apropos a slighted system of inhalation sadness &
return (gifts to me my world   each exhalation)

we have made many beds about the house for sleep   we have made them as decla-
rations resistances   love notes to sleep   each night a retreat a martyr a regularity
we sneak or heavy stone stagger to whichever area of suburban carpet will nestle our
need to

leave this—

              which is beautiful

unchartered & ergo frightening   frightened & angry at doctors who do & do not do
a continual relation to devotion to the next specialist   little circles of light all Emer-
sonian expanding us all bed bath & way

beyond   has any one ever drowned in light or love or development of a light il-
luminant   Dear there is an inner light for certain & an outer coat reflective but
also there is a like & unlike child & between them   I believe shades of child

              & my child

so it's clear to me

so it's clear to me
flesh is a window open to rot
& meat for the air
of this world is fetid
bodies of menwomen swollen in air
in the square   swollen meat

there is day & there is night
a position of the window
for each to press at the pane

attraction   a bare action
something from bone

Difficult Head, 1995

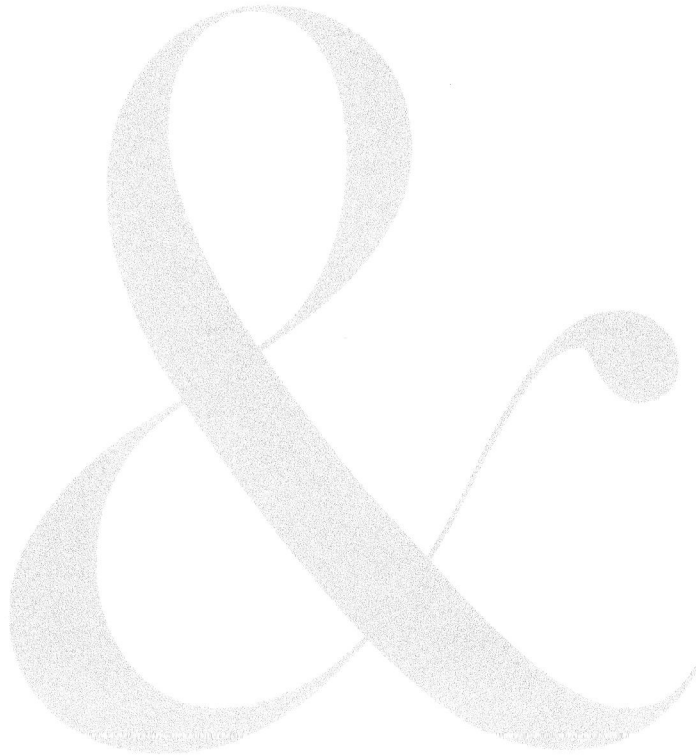

g-tube, lightning & excursion

1.

after our daughter was diagnosed & after failed
interventions & after medical devices sprouted up around her crib

they dug a passageway between her belly & her stomach
& liquids poured through & she was nourished

& on that very afternoon
our house was struck by lightning

since then

have I ever not known luminosity
ever felt the stupor

                              the lightening   less surprising
                    was humorous even   fire burst out the oven door
                        the instance   you leaping aside   was antic

a surgeon bores a hole
in Maya's abdomen
our mouths   our magnitude   closed up

close-up:

the machine's beeping & churning
interrupted by a jolt a flash
a bleak beating or blast in the universe & no vantage
is ever the same & I wanted it to be a lightening

not a bruise   not another eye

this is which is unclear   we were unclear   & urgent

sticky with sudden formula   crib & wail & infant
glass shards   lightbulbs   florets on the blonde fir floor

her mouth was closed
I thought it was a moment &
& then a pre-moment

but the passing of her closure isn't yet

intervention occurs because a specialist

is well-versed in probable ways
that shouldn't happen & do

a pre-hour arcs seamlessly into
mnemonics

an arc & an arc & the motion escalates
into aperture

lightning then is intervention is
diametric

for one hour it rains
reversal of swelter

white & red lights swirling
while firemen wand the house for errant heat
we wait in the firemen's truck

there's a hole in my heart
there's a murmur

toddler assumes both mobility & age
& is only half appropriate then for my faltering girl
whee ohhh whee ooh circles the son's little mouth
transfixed as rain reflects the light   drops
streaming down the pane

peeping is a way of gazing from the belly

2.

I am so well versed in the day
where you go to go how it goes gangly

I go on

I have to be careful about going on &
on
because I go on & on
I never stop the on

don't I   go on   dear
go on

the way you translate it
I'm responsible   I did go on

but didn't you go off

collaboration or daughter
you liked what I made
the materials were your's
the directions part mine & part from an ad
& you liked what I made
or you didn't   & took it back
the materials   then we were
unhappening
        as a unit

as a unit an hour is post & it is
the fourth of July
we remember
the Fourth of July

but didn't you go off
go off

I don't   in the igniting   know your interior
but words do   words being exterior

they fly back into the chest   interred
all the plosives off the tongue
afire

you smoked pot to keep you grounded
in the hour & to dilute the intensity of the hour
& to draw you an arc

I said to you

I will draw you an ark

Chiron's job is serious business   I said
ferrying essentially time from time
seamless   & a crossing back

to myself

youacloudsodensesolowyouacloudsodensesolowyouacloudsodyouacloudsodens-
esolowyouacloudsodensesolow youacloudsodensesolowyouacloudsodensesolow
youacloudsodensesolowyouacloudsodensesolo

soliloquy

before this   motherwife job
what pre-req
what resume

an *achron*—

3.

we'd imagined equal rest
equal   opening

would our child open

we'd imagined
engagement

　　as miracle & practice

4.

in a post-hour recalling a sordid vantage from what might have been readily remembered   I doubt it   the past hour   the door revolving   I doubt it   a revolver   now the hour is a pre-hour: doubt   I can only tell you for certain that ghosts were the mayors of summer & now the snows have blanketed all the fires licked   it is char & white   thesis & anti-thesis

so it is clear to me

what you cannot speak   probably cannot speak you

probably

I travel I-25 from the suburbs in the morning

in the distance   snow & wind & wire
Cheyenne   & in the night back again
watchingly silent   two coins in my palm
buffalo & wind

we left the pre-hour for the Hour & what must be done
is the adoption of understanding transactions

one(s) to terminate
one(s) essential

the way to communicate from afar

Iassureyou
Iassureyou
Iassureyou

I have recognized every hour of everyday
for as long as the recent recent I recall

so I am acclimated
                    well-versed

        versal

            I can sing any song the day sings

but you can predict what I wanted to eat

                        in a future   we are unattached

                        & therefore unrecognizable
                        one to another

                        but there you are   waving
                        & we are not yet met

                        this is not another country   one of us is in
                        another country

5.

a thousand years in god's sight are like a day that has just gone by
one day is as one-thousand years & one-thousand years is like a day

& so it was with us in moments days passed & in the days years

not yet ready
to unknow   & knowing
one of us was in another country

we made travel plans

my world his world
a third world travel plan

6.

preparation

it is my will to live in the future   but forever the clock forbids it   adamant   I
act as I am preparing or I have gathered the supplies for another hour   now
there is nothing in the breadbasket   someone close to me breaks a stick   now
the mirror is dark as the sod is dark   I stare out   when I am past this   &
hourly   I will say *there is something I forgot*   something casual I'd ignored   I
hadn't had it in the pre-hour & I won't have it now

    daily bread

I say *oh* &   *I forgot* &   *there was something obvious*
somewhat casually I say &   *you can't get that here*

    you say
           no you can't

as if the bread is always flown in from elsewhere   as if no one will be alive
during the tour

These   the things we'll carry:

umbrella wipee sun-in sunscreen tampons add-ons
sunhat   sundress son's ID   daughter's ID doxcylamine eyewear
iPad   inky pens   scissors anti-drowning alert device Rx
extra shoes   batteries excedrin extra cables tire tubes   g-tubes
nylon rope   slingshot   synthroid slackline money for the ferry

when the hour comes will it be awake

say we are in the post-   say a book of this pre- is no longer accurate   patience
is long   accepting there are many significant patients is helpful   for the liv-
ing   this is also misleading   in route you might behave so   so misleading-
ly   when an idea cannot fit any longer into context & you are the idea   on
tour   entanglement ensues

                                        then a vantage

when are we leaving the hour
this hour   we left   still in a pre-hour

I am assuring you how absent the hour

you want me to say *rush*   but we left

some of us left in our bodies
some of us left our minds in our bodies
someofusstayedtopractise*piecemealnecrosis*
some of us left on our left foot   & others left later

we are betrothed   as it is betrothed
to us   our plot of land & the pipes & wires
that poke at us

                                        they too are betrothed to us

7.

excursion

here we are now   hey this will be us   the materials part yours part mine the
directions are part of an ark & you like what we made & you don't take it back
& here we happen

penchants for meat cakes, Oranjeboom & ear infections

            the hour promised was not permanence
            permanence is not an anti-surprise hour

            anti-surprise when our hour
            arrives &
                aside from the scenery   the alteration
            is musical
                  this is not a practice
            dependent on the land

            however   I bring my supplies

            send for scissors   forgot the scissors

8.

imagine equal rest
equal   opening

does the lightning open

   you

    there

you are
the child

      opening
    lightening

   pressuring

aperture   for miracle & practice

the gardener in March immobile

the gardener

      (in March   immobile
        winter still   here not a crocus
        not a thaw   )

wilts

twenty four tomato vines   eggplants
pea plants tomatillos turnips

twenty four tomato vines   eggplants
pea plants tomatillos turnips

in the spring he left

twenty four tomato vines   eggplants
pea plants tomatillos turnips

columbines   Johnny jump ups
twenty four tomato vines   eggplants
front steps   candy for the daughter tomatillos turnips

twenty four tomato vines   eggplants
pea plants tomatillos turnips

twenty four tomato vines   eggplants
pea plants tomatillos turnips

sd. trim your tree
twenty four tomato vines   eggplants
sd. kill yr. weeds
pea plants tomatillos turnips

twenty four tomato vines   eggplants
pea plants tomatillos turnips

twenty four tomato vines   eggplants
pea plants tomatillos turnips

that was last spring   barely April

26

we ask for more   we have
small plots

(with what you have do more)

bodies or gardens   the L.   raises each
seed & soul grow   higher

the land is a pleasant neighbor

(loving as himself
                    =
           goats weed)

if the gardener is my neighbor
his name is Greenhouse John   if
if I loved my neighbor
my neighbor = myself

like if by wilt
if by my neighbor
meant if I had loved
John like myself
if all neighbors were not as neighbors
but my selves

a neighbor   as if

if I had myself to wilt a little

or take your yoke   my neighbor unto me
if I Moses had held your arms
if I a greenhouse in my heart had built

had Love loved a sunroom

(recall an evening   a barren blue planter

    &

we'd talked about lavender

    lemon balm

lamb's ears

                sensory things

           for my sad low-lying dtr.

 you sd.
you'd look around

    sd. the greenhouse…   goddamnit so many

sd. god
           's tossing them away   sd. now

wouldn't she enjoy

       petting them)

(will)

beehives for the daughter   the son
(always for the daughter)   wrenches & hammers

for wife
    I'm sorry
  your imaginary beehive   it is real
  stingers

        neighbor not myself
   is love
          man&wife is one

  I'm sorry

          Love's

beehives   surprise
more apples than ever the covenant wanted

(so mythical)   you're off

trekking an ancient mission

in the underworld's old garden

to emerge shinning

                              honeycombs

in your grip

                 lamb's ears

seals are what bullets ought be

sooted sheen & mooring drift hymn

casing dissolves to driftwood
casket to gunmetal wave

if there is an angel of death
there's pontoon grace to land her

ash is a color of the mourning sea

seals are what bullets ought be

buoyed lash & slowly lute song

bell & horn atop an inlet
a shatter in a barrel

measured   warning   rhythmic

Hangende Figur, 1989

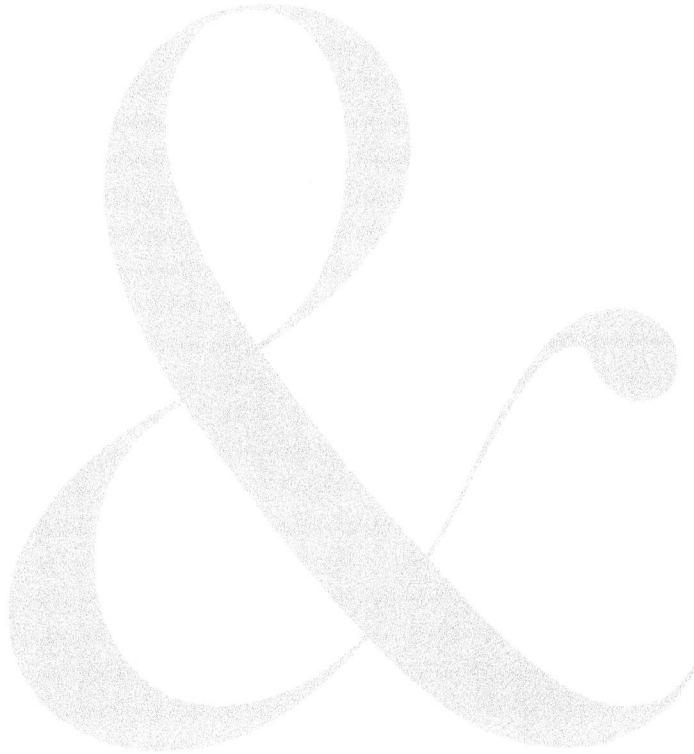

recovery

I too am a part of the snowy junipers & the street lamp & the evening

blackbird suspended between rooftops & birches & ashes & of the man
tugged by his sweatered dogs over the ice

       orange the spilled moon

emerging into the immersive ethereal

lying in bed   Miyazawa on my mind

      I am a part of the core of the world
      surgeried & waiting

apparition from below   alighting on surface   leaving the sky above

unbeaten by the rain   unbeaten by the snow   strong of body

in landscape submerged   November & the quickly settling light
forwarding into the steppes of mountains

                it pulls equally away from us all

dawn is isolatory except for blackbirds   redbirds
birches where they have long been building slowly

Sasha knitts a cloak for her daughter's Komodo dragon

stepping in from the fields' bright & barren apple trees
John & Sue Ellen with dachshunds
now brushing off the thistle

              free of desire   never angry

Mike already at his law firm & stepped early in poetry   Mulberry below
Canyon crossing through
he makes robust decisions

lying in bed   Miyazawa in my mind

    does Micah put the war behind his head where he cannot see it

I too am a part of the core of the world

the seems of my spine glued & stitched   I rest

turning the blinds   Matthew rises to see Doug   & the icy slush
Doug   assessing the uncleanliness of our court
fractured sidewalks leaking gutters

                              redbirds above him chirping
in the cherry choke of which they too are a part

          even Doug is a part

waking & resting in the day & idleness & flurry
rustled by inherent wind & let to still again

                              neither praised nor a bother

I want to rake my heart & her neighboring vessels
back to the places they fell
swept up in the cry of the snow owl

such is the person I wish to be

                    Miyazawa on my mind

something from bone

something from bone
to heal the bone   soothing
from Icthus for me
open the window   & the sea
pulls in   boil the water & the gills
pluck out & fling open
the bone   lick clean the marrow
& scatter all loss in the sea

Pointing Figure II, 1986

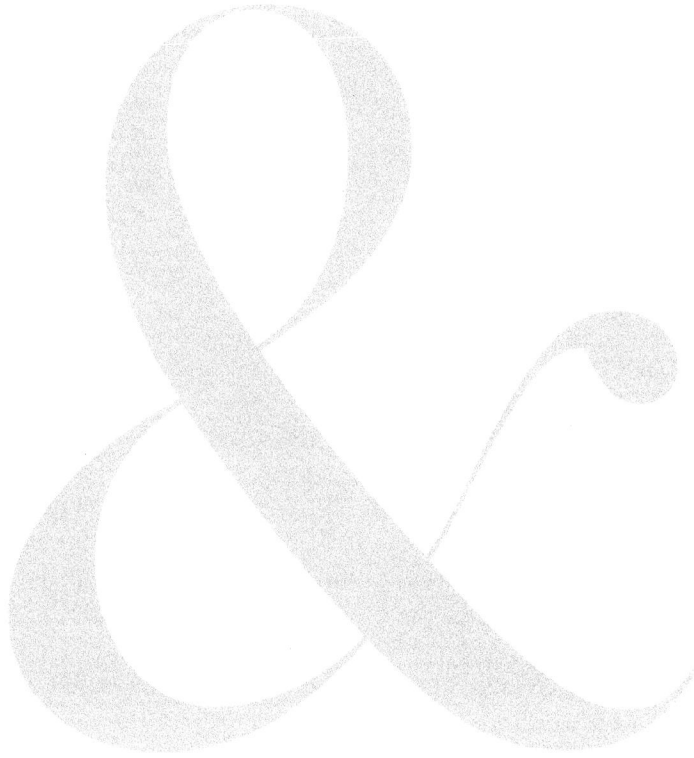

bough

"little gray toad of a heart flopping
weakly here or there in his chest"
                              —Ray Bradbury

& then there is that night when all around, all around you hear the cracking
of tree limbs, one by one, from the trees. At first it is one here & one there,
& then it is four then five then nine then thirty, until all the limbs impress
like raccoon prints, shatter like crystals in the blue October snow & you are
the last limb on the oak & you liken for the lamplight to lift you down gentle
from your grip upon the wet & leafy sky.

Long before you press into the firmament, you will have forgotten there ever
was a wimple or other branches or breach or low & loamy soil beneath the
crystalline wild.

night   allaround
      night

      limbs cracking

first one here/there   & there

  4   5   9   & 30

limb crystals shatter

      raccoon prints impress

a   blue October snow   &   You
                                last   limb

                            the oak   on

& liken for lamplight

    lift me down gentle   my grip
    clings

      oh wet & leafy sky

there was ever wimple   branch or breach
low & loamy   the soil churns
beneath a glassy trill

lamplight on snow branch of oak limb
over wet leaves snow

in background   sound of cracking
in air   fingernail moon above branch

being that lets the present
such that this is
hues & weights
framed in landscape

impression of raccoon prints
October's blueness of gleaming snow

loamy soil beneath

Conditions:

& then there is   all around   all around
From   at first   here/there   until
the last   long before
     you will have

                    beneath

                                        Bones:

Nightallhearcrack   limbonetreeoneherethere   fourfiveninethirtyall   limbsshatter
                    Impresscrystalsracoonprints   blueoctober

$N_2 A_8 L_{12} C O_4 T_6 F S_4 R_1 P I_1 B_4 Y_1 M$
$_2 D_1 G_2 W_3 E_1$

après toi, le deluge cochineal

crimson around things
delicious   luscious

wheel barrow to calla lip

it seemed a fine coffer
carnine in winter snow   we were curious
how we hadn't known   retrospected
we'd been left in it   fainting there while the skilled moons
circled by lilies   ice crowns   pine bough
pressed stiffly into our grave

russian doll red wall
the way we start a fire

in the year of solutions
we painted it red

we bought it red
our friends & we   spoke red

we couldn't stop the ferrous wake

drifts slight enough for hibernation
wide enough to conceal the slope

slept heavily

asphyxiated the chirring roots

the intermezzo of two lives   *près* and *après* of both

arise

red mouthed
cherried

the year of solution

if children half grey & the dead fence remains
tall & near   if only in low tones & on their hands
with a startling sky dropping parachutes eye mites
if there are flames in the shapes of marching bands &
carmine birch   then could there be an invitation
a new ceremony   on the lawn

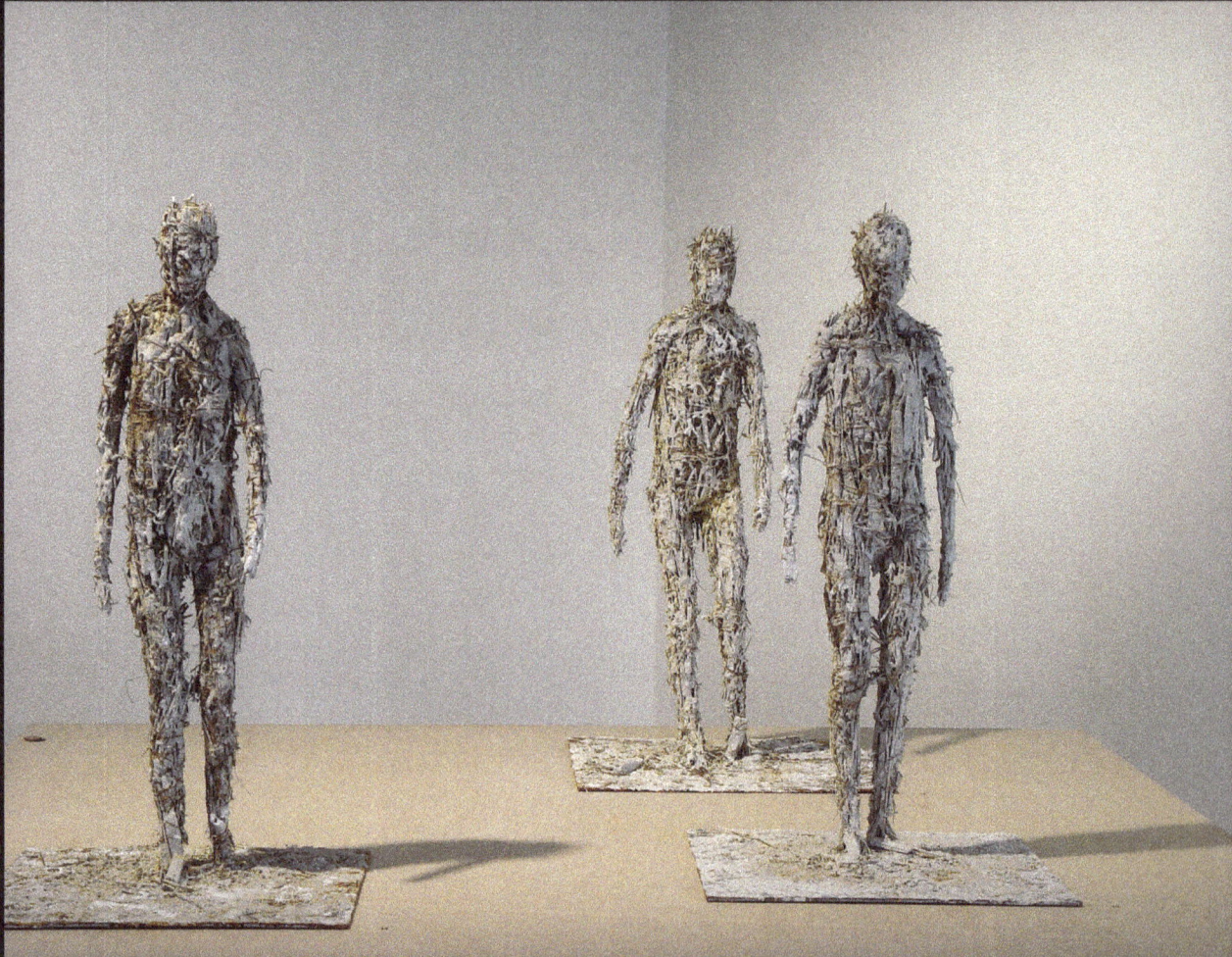

Dancing Figures I, II, & III, 2007

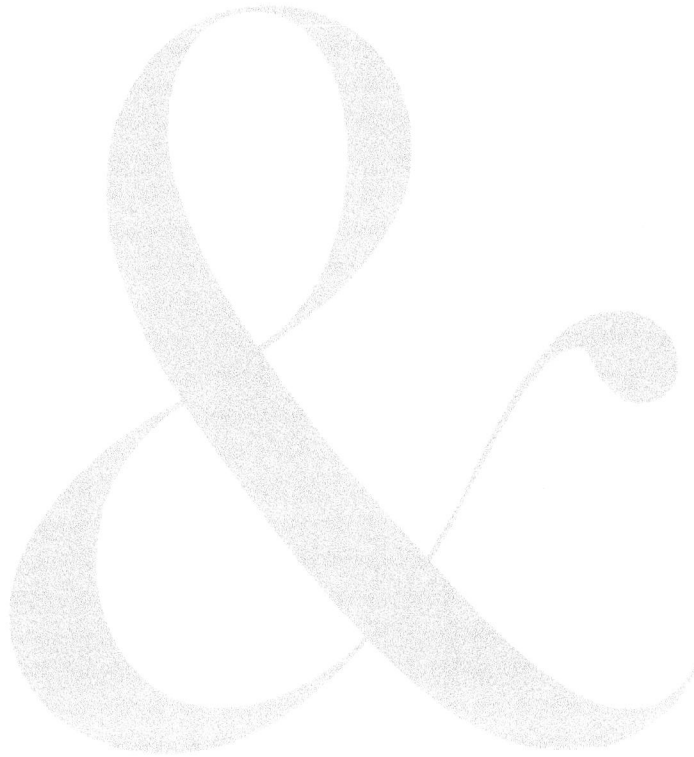

reconnaissance

Earth photographed from 37,000 km away   in space   is most
most general most graphic   it is a most physical form:

                                                    man contemplates
man outside of man

                    maximum   general
                    _____   _____
                    generalization   most

                                                in superlatives

life contemplates itself   from beyond itself
                    fundamentally

    the face of the first woman bends over a mirror of water
    contemplating her reflection

                              the face in the mirror is always
                              a fraction
                              of a second
                              younger than the real face

man is the only
animal producing
art
      the only animal
                    contemplating himself
                          from outside   himself

                              (this is such bullshit
                              consider the bowerbird
                              praxis creator of
                              a ponderous—bottle cap
                              snail shell blue bead twine
                              & pelt—nest)

          art = namely a man's
                          feelings

the feeling of time is the strangest art & 1st
material from which the matrix is breeched

matrix / mater   mother's tricks   *vis-a-vis*

you can't make something out of nothing noyoucan't

the 1st fish throws itself
above a water's surface

a moment

& the fish contemplates

itself

from the outside

(I often contradict myself: man & fish are one
fishman

I am on the outside

manna made)

the feeling of time   so strong so tensile   it moves (leaps crawls how does it move)
out from the matrix

     mother clay

the reflection of the fish in the pond
the woman in the mirror

always the real face is a fraction of a second   older /

                            tethered /

                            exposed /

    (in between
    the real
    & the reflected

          freeing & freezing & fleeting

    time's feeling / the feeling of time)

I am troubled by this photo—
        Earth & yet & also 37,000 km away
                & I with my one eye
there it goes
        the myth   the drawn globe   hierarchies

                              I cannot claim beyond perception

continents are as sea snails on the floor of an aerial sea   roiling
roiling in roseate cloud's magnificent suspense
sub-aerial eerie waves   diaphanous
azure-auroxed contingents among the circle of the total horizon

                     MAN

he does not dwell
on the surface
of the globe

                  no   man

is an interior   from an interior stratum of the matrix of the globe   *man*

                  sometimes I ask myself   if
                  the feeling of time   is not
                  by any means time as such
                  & also if by no means
                  time as such is nothing
                    nothing but a feeling
                              matrix of sentiments

                                    sediment

he could be called sub-aerial
he could   some creature from under the clouds
some sub

        sub [nimbus   imber obscurus   cirrus   cummulos   stratus   urban]

        substrate & I have always been moved by fish leaping over the waters

this is not man's feeling

once a young man
in a town oceanic   his blood   watching it from outside the glass
& gazing   already a moment younger than   already from
at his own reflection   the outside seizing in   i wept   his pain
saw himself older   on my side of the pane   streetside
just a fraction &
tattoo-ed himself   fishes left over the water not considering
all flying fish   themselves a moment
wing tip to wing tip
circum tri- & bicep
aerial & arm bent

        this is more than
        art is more than

        ne plus ultra

        a man's feelings

GENESIS

fish over the water leap

                                        is a perpetual phenomenon

I have always been moved

                              [no fixed date
                              humanity]

birth through the length of time measured & nomend by & in perpetual
statistical & qualitative growth

cosmonauts leaping above the air

                                        convert to lucid greatness
                                        leaps of winged fish over the sea

so long as
humanity over heat leads to birth
over time

recurrently
                (draw diagram here
                  a mano)

                                 this is a contemplation
                                 from outside & an insignia
                                 of evolution

                                            simultaneously

a photograph of Earth
                        37,000 km of vision   of measure

   locus of humanity's history unfolding

      this is the net total   this the genesis
this the Aleph mathmatical point from which the old magi now modern mathman claims

this whole universe
can be contemplated
in the entirety
of its senses
in its entire
physical beauty

in simultaneity

I am tried

  —I swear—

I am tried

by my happiness for science

science materializes [at last!] a feeling

poetry has had since her birth

poetry has always contemplated man from

outside

  —& do not believe that I'm not happy—

I want so much   to say it

to speak I am happy

to have lived in this time of

    et cetera…

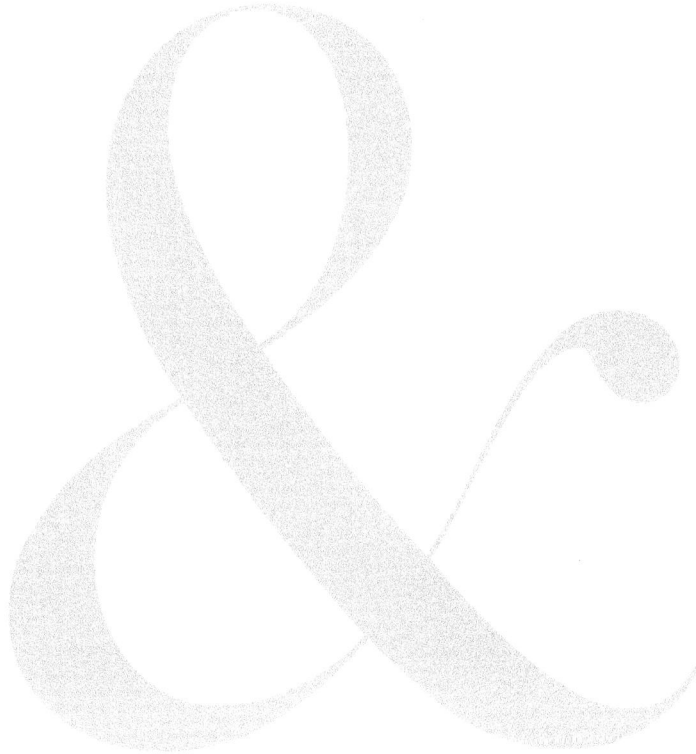

Lord knows I'd die

in war
in flood
in embarrassment

in adultery   in a city
in a lake of meat-slurry   in a snake-
drawn carriage   in a glass house
the 26th dead mouse   in sub-
zero thaw
               if I lost

a child   if i lost a child
twice   in flames taller than the lilac tree
of my youth on South First

I won't die without   You

              Lord   knows

I'd die in kool-aide   in Waco
in braids   with or without first aide
in Harlem   in a six-day AWP in a Seventh
Day Adventist church   in a second
eye surgery

             in a second

Lord knows

I'd pull up my drawers

I'd die

over

not beyond but done—its o
the house crawls full of bees
by the waters in the arbor   yes where all our currency of blame was lost
    a small small agent built a ship
        over & over *sure   sure*   we were *sure*
she took the sidewalk   took jewelry took fall   took
information from our ears   and *sure*
sure   we withered in our house full of bees
by the water   less the sidewalk   by the crawling currency of lostness
& shore   with all our jewels

lameless

I am in love with bees & sidewalks &
jewelry in fall I am in love with ships &
ship builders & I am sure of my house in
the parterre with bees am sure of small
conversations and currency & sure of my
ear near currents of water & sure that the
sidewalk crawls over lost agents & blame
I am in love with the effort of bees with
less yeses & lost formations & yes I am
the love of blameless our arbor

don't build   ship

                shore up the agent of blame
& ship her   the bees are assured
of fall   the swift currency
of water over conversations
& jeweled sidewalks in parterres of effortless plot

you fall   because you are lost   less
& lost   this fall   this agent
of surety   of blame effortless   & bees
falling sideways on waterwalks
assure you of lost currency   of
shoreless lost ships   of
                        over in my
arbor lot

the bees blamed less every year
is over
                        over in my
garden
jewelryless agents crawl fallen
sidewalks
the water cages over
                so don't build
ship

blame in the bee house

build effort   build blame   build your own plot hive
crawl the sidewalk to it   build anything
but don't loose it   and when you do
                                                         blame me

blame me for your ardor   for lost bees   for currency
of ears in conversation waterlogged amidst the ships

blame me   for   I built them
the currency of   plot houses of crawling conversation
fear ships   agent blame & her jewelry

so build a bee fall   build yesterday lost
build your blame house in your garden lot
lease it to the lost   the shipless   the small & blaming
                                                    & blame me

blame me or build me yesterday less lame built

time   again

poppies   between
crimming

                                                  silencing

                                          again dimming
                              to drown (the we others face)

                                                  however:
                                        we lie
                                                          little
                                            skyface
                          to churchyard face

          (fxn:)?

again: silent lower eye   landscaped
                    ((in/e)scape)together   so old
                                                          fullyright

          under two two

              "1"   +   (she+1)

                  +

              (forming two minute halves)
              _____

              agained: 3 + 2 = 4   well

all know

        & love well   trees names

the *of*

                    wherein *ravine*
                 (ousted & timed)

        ends

        (the the)

bury the guise

in the whet of the sooted dove's wing
in the town square of love's dusty breast

bury the hatchet

>   bury the grudge
>   the seed
>   the forgiveness that bloomed then rotted
>   the scorecard   the bulb
>   the need for meat
>   the blackball blackboard burnt heart

>   the need for meat which rots in the square

hunt it out
blowout the horns

I expect   not one is doomed

except accept

if one weaves

>   —with or without intention—

in their loins
>   death's third chord

E*roica,* E minor

>   bury your hero
>   here

après John

to say   he swallowed
the grave   alludes also to his weight
his *joie de vivre*

                      [joke #x ends with a bounce]
    swallows

    air & bullet swallow-er

I have to write a poem as big as him
                         I have to
write it with *largess*
    & *revolution*

he was revolting   fragmented

had fatshort gnomish fingers

loved Virgil &

           he had grande humors
swallowed lakes

& when I say *him* I say *&* *&* *&*

I say past   he saw past

it was such a small urn
for such a large *&*

you come home to the rest of your life

you come

it's fall

an enigma of embers & etching

you've come   home to rest

but its life

its etched & re-scribed & the embers falling

why've you come to this nest?

you've lit it aflame

love's wretching

the love of your nest
is embering   anymores love's

embering

fervor for the rest of your life

there / here

nests & the span

between leaves is alluring

light & the leaves alluring

embers in your eyes love

lighting the leaves

you've come lighting leaves as if

you've a flame suit

your nesting in embers

as if you have only one flame

love committed a flame in your nest

as if you were amber as if in drought

the leaves & the embers are call cards

you've come to a life with call cards

little nests burning   you've left

each thorny doorstep bouqueted in blaze

each dozen embered

you came home

alighting on anger & rattling leaves

you came home
    to torches   arduous eyes

so you left
    & you left your bouquet

as if you were careful   burning
bouquets positioned on doorsteps
thorn steps   fire cards

as if it were fetching

                        hurt one   come home to rest

                     it's fall   your nests are enigmae
                        of etching   come home

                     to the rest   of the rest   of your life

Konkav Figur, 1989

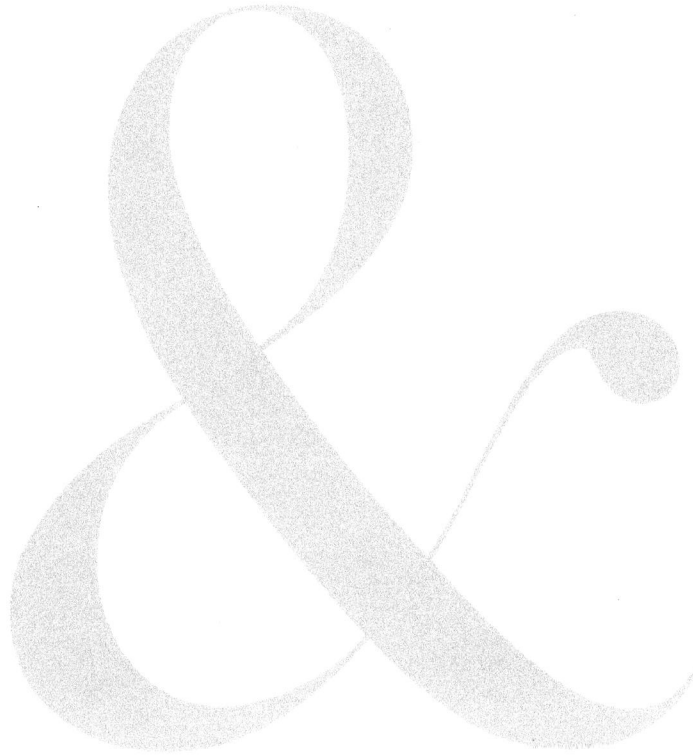

flame falls as falls the world down

       everyone flailing deepstep

the tongue   the hair   the leg
the scent   the door   the rain
the sightless

in stranger's breath the jewel opens
to last within the stars

       everyone calls *we're paint breath all in all*

stars deep line
turned signal love
fences call the world to leave

       blinded lie

the sad love   the car sky   the poultice meat
the into eyes   the glove

       mine eyes that closed within sigh eyes

there's love's
driver

icthus & bone   kind   the stranger's part paints stranger's stars

            everyone choosing deepstep

the hot-herb   the darkened room   the breath
the shift   the hour   the driven dogs

I'll with meat eyes make
I'll in darkened room
I'll the plot to shift the stars

            I'll   the streak   the lungs   the moon lane

I'll to morning's mourning love
blear   the boneman   a vineyard now

we're the mullein & the river & the driven arbor dogs

            public places pale the skin

            play the line   the loosened glove   the then for what

            for dreams   dimmed eyes   evening's flame

yes

                              & there's you still thrill hour of the would to love

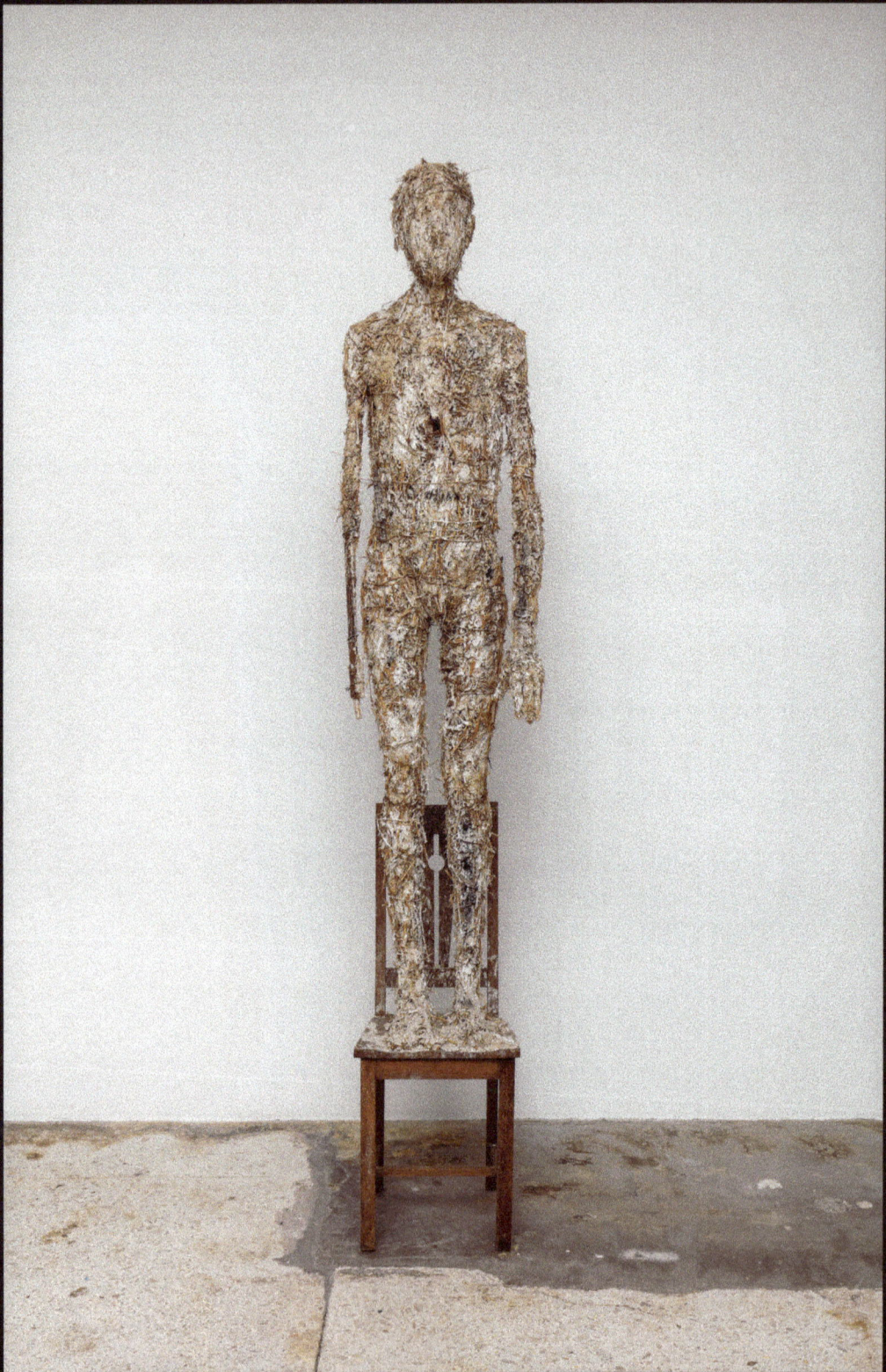

Figure on Chair, 1993

Notes

the gardener in March immobile: for my neighbor John, who brought plants & laughter & nearly fixed our sprinkler system (b. 1962, d. 2011, suicide)

recovery: lines in sage taken from Kenji Miyazawa's Poem "Ame ni mo makezu" translated by David Sulz

reconnaissance: engages & takes great liberties with Nichita Stanescu's poem, "contemplation of man from outside himself" translated into English by Romanian-born painter & dear friend, Marius Lehene

après John: for John Biasiolli. I'm sorry I missed your call. (b. 1977, d. 2008, age 31, suicide)

flame falls as falls the world down: originally a Tzarian exercise using texts from C. D. Wright's "The Crossing Counts" & "David Bowie's Modern Love." Wright and Bowie both died in 2018.

Photo Credits: James Sullivan

About the Author

Aby Kaupang is the author of *& there's you still thrill hour of the world to love*, *Radiant Tether*, *NOS, disorder not otherwise specified* (with Matthew Cooperman), *Little "g" God Grows Tired of Me*, and multiple other collections. She holds master's degrees in creative writing and occupational therapy. Employed outside of academia, she practices as an occupational therapist and nurse's aide specializing in treating neurodivergent and special needs children. Aby lives in Fort Collins, Colorado, where she assists in organizing an annual book festival, hosts the reading series, Every Eye, and has served as Poet Laureate. More information can be found at abykaupang.com.

Photograph of the author by Aby Kaupang.
Used by persmission.

Free Verse Editions

Edited by Jon Thompson

Spine by Carolyn Guinzio

Spool by Matthew Cooperman

Strange Antlers by Richard Jarrette

A Suit of Paper Feathers by Nate Duke

Summoned by Guillevic, trans. by Monique Chefdor & Stella
    Harvey

Sunshine Wound by L. S. Klatt

System and Population by Christopher Sindt

These Beautiful Limits by Thomas Lisk

They Who Saw the Deep by Geraldine Monk

The Thinking Eye by Jennifer Atkinson

This History That Just Happened by Hannah Craig

An Unchanging Blue: Selected Poems 1962–1975 by Rolf Dieter
    Brinkmann, trans. by Mark Terrill

Under the Quick by Molly Bendall

Verge by Morgan Lucas Schuldt

The Visible Woman by Allison Funk

The Wash by Adam Clay

We'll See by Georges Godeau, trans. by Kathleen McGookey

What Stillness Illuminated by Yermiyahu Ahron Taub

Winter Journey [Viaggio d'inverno] by Attilio Bertolucci, trans.
    by Nicholas Benson

Wonder Rooms by Allison Funk

www.ingramcontent.com/pod-product-compliance
Lightning Source LLC
Chambersburg PA
CBHW061415090426
42742CB00024B/3471

9 7 8 1 6 4 3 1 7 3 5 8 0